GREENE, CAROL   02/14/92
CARING FOR OUR WATER
(1) 1991 *BRODART
0135 04 317597 01 0   (IC=1)

B013504317597010B

J
363.739
Gre   Greene, Carol

         Caring for our
         water

DUE DATE

D1303376

(6-9)

APR 9 2

WITHDRAWN

SOULE BRANCH
Onondaga County
Public Library

101 SPRINGFIELD ROAD
SYRACUSE, NY 13214

PROPERTY OF
ONONDAGA COUNTY PUBLIC LIBRARY

"Whoever wilfully detains any . . . property
belonging to any public or incorporated library . . .
for thirty days after notice . . . to return the
same . . . shall be punished by a fine not less than
one nor more than twenty-five dollars, or by im-
prisonment in jail not exceeding six months . . ."

N Y S Education Law
Section 265

Caring for Our
WATER

Carol Greene

CARING FOR OUR EARTH

ENSLOW PUBLISHERS, INC.

Bloy St. & Ramsey Ave.   P.O. Box 38
Box 777   Aldershot
Hillside, N.J. 07205   Hants GU12 6BP
U.S.A.   U.K.

Copyright © 1991 by Enslow Publishers, Inc.

All rights reserved.

No part of this book may be reproduced by any means
without the written permission of the publisher.

Library of Congress Cataloging-in-Publication Data

Greene, Carol.
    Caring for our water / Carol Greene.
       p. cm.—(Caring for our earth)
    Includes index.
    Summary: Simple text and illustrations describe different
ecological problems relating to water, and suggest ways to preserve
this resource.
    ISBN 0-89490-356-X
    1. Water conservation—Juvenile literature. 2. Water—Juvenile
literature. [1. Water. 2. Water conservation. 3. Environmental
protection. 4. Pollution.] I. Title. II. Series: Greene, Carol.
Caring for our earth.
TD388.G74 1991   91-2683
363.73'94—dc20   CIP
                                                         AC

Printed in the United States of America

10 9 8 7 6 5 4 3 2 1

Photo Credits: Margaret Cooper, pp. 6, 8, 14; Metropolitan St. Louis Sewer
District, pp. 19, 24, 27; Sarah Nelson, pp. 4, 17; R. Roger Pryor, pp. 11
(bottom), 25; United Nations, p. 21; United States Department of Agricul-
ture, p. 11 (top); United States Fish & Wildlife Service, p. 23; Webster Groves
Fire Department, p. 12; WHO photo by Jean Mohr, p. 16.

Cover Photo: Clifford Greene

Contents

This is fresh water. You can drink it—if it is clean.

What Is It?

The earth is mostly
made of it.
Your body is mostly
made of it.
All living things
need it to stay alive.
What is it? Water.

Water covers much
of the earth.

This is salt water.
You can't drink it.

But most of it

is in the oceans.

It is salty and you

can't drink it.

Water without salt

is called fresh water.

You can find it

in rivers and streams,

lakes and ponds.

But most fresh water

is frozen into ice

in cold parts of the world.

So people can use

only a small part

of all the water

in the world.

But that small part

is enough—if we

take good care of it.

Animals need clean water, too.

Why Is Water Important?

All plants, animals,
and people need
water to live.
Without water, they
cannot use their food
or get rid of wastes.

If you went more than
a week without water,
you would die.

People also use water
to grow plants for food.
It takes a lot of water
to grow a crop
of wheat or corn.

Much of this water
comes from rain.
But in dry places,
people must bring
water to their crops.

Some plants and animals
make their home in water.
Fish, whales, dolphins,
water lilies, and cattails
will soon die out of water.

Without water, these apple trees would not grow.

Water also cleans things.
People use it to
wash dishes and clothes,
take showers and baths,
brush teeth, flush toilets,
and many other things.

Factories use a lot of water.
They use it to clean things
and to make things.

Water lilies make
their home in water.

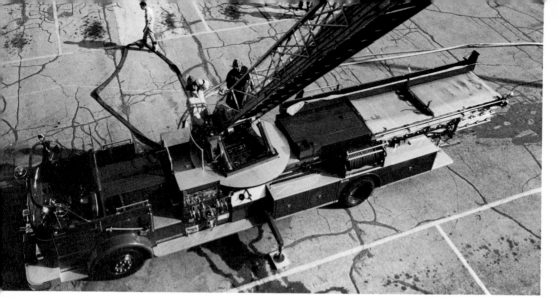

People use water
in many ways.
Here is one
important way.

But mostly they use it

to cool things, such as steel.

People also use water

to make power.

Then they use the power

to make heat or light

or to run machines.

Sometimes people move

things on water.

Ships carry goods
across the ocean.
Barges carry goods
up and down rivers.

Water is important
for all these reasons.
But it is also important
because it is beautiful
—and fun.

People can swim in it
or sail or ski.
They can stand still
and look at a waterfall or a
lake at sunset.

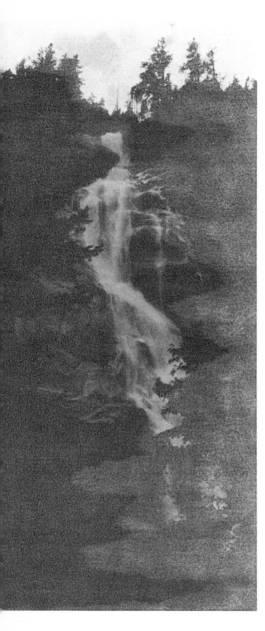

Some people paint
pictures of water.
Others write music
or poems about it.
They show how beautiful
water is.

Some water is
very beautiful.

14

What Can Happen to Water?

Water can get dirty.

This happens when
pollutants from factories
get into it.
Pollutants are harmful
things left over after
burning or making something.

Pollutants from factories make water dirty.

Other factory pollutants can
get into the air.
There they mix with rain
and fall to earth again.

This is called acid rain.
It harms plants and trees.
It kills fish and
other water animals.
It can even harm
buildings and bridges.

Water can get dirty
from farm wastes, too.

Pollutants from this factory
can get into the air
and fall to earth
in rain or snow.

Some farmers use
too many pest-killers
to kill weeds and insects.
They use too many fertilizers
to make crops grow tall.

These things mix
with rain or snow.
They get into rivers,
lakes, and streams
and make the water dirty.

Water can also get
dirty from sewers.
Sewer water is full of
wastes, garbage, and soap.

Sometimes people clean
sewer water, so it
can be used again.
But sometimes they just
let it run into
rivers, lakes, or oceans.

Sometimes people let dirty sewer water run into rivers,
lakes, or oceans.

People also spill things
into the water by accident.
Ships spilling oil are
a big problem right now.

Dirty water spreads diseases.
Sometimes people die
from drinking it.
In some places, people
have run out of
clean, fresh water.

Dirty water can also
kill plants, fish, birds,
and other animals.

These children must get
their drinking water
from a muddy puddle.

It can make our
rivers, lakes, and oceans
ugly and smelly.

What Can We Do?

The earth can have
clean water if people
stop dumping things into it.

People can make laws
to stop factories from
dumping pollutants.
Factories can find
better ways to get rid
of their pollutants.

The earth can have clean water if people are careful.

Farmers can use safe ways
to kill pests and
make crops grow tall.

People can clean up
all the water and wastes
that run through sewers.

People can also
be more careful.

Water from sewers
is cleaned here,
so it can be used again.

Beavers built their dam in this clean water.

They can build better
ships to carry oil.
They can try to
use less oil, too.

Cleaning up our water
and keeping it clean
will take hard work.
It will cost money.
But the earth must
have clean water.

What Can You Do?

You can help
keep water clean, too.
Here are some things
that you can do.

1. Don't throw litter
   in or around water.
   (Don't throw litter anywhere
   except into trash bins.)

2. Don't let the water run
   while you brush your teeth.
   Just turn it on to wet
   your brush and to rinse.
   This will save clean water.

Tell your parents or teacher if you see a dripping faucet.
Dripping faucets waste a lot of clean water.

3. Don't let the water run
    to get yourself a cold drink.
    Keep a bottle of water
    in the refrigerator for drinks.
    You'll save more clean water.

4. Take short showers
    instead of baths.
    Short showers use
    less clean water, too.

5. Draw a picture or
    write a poem about water.
    Show what you have done
    to your family and friends.

Words to Know

acid rain—Rain, snow, or sleet with pollutants in it.

fresh water—Water without much salt in it.

ice—Frozen water.

ocean—A large body of salt water.

oil—A greasy liquid that can be burned.

pollutant (poh-LOOT-ent)—A thing left over after burning or making something. It is harmful to the earth.

salt water—Water with a lot of salt in it.

sewer—A large pipe, most often under the ground, that carries away water and wastes.

water—A liquid that falls from the clouds and covers much of the earth.

Index

About the Author

Carol Greene is the author of about 100 books for children. She has also worked as a children's editor and a teacher of writing for children. Ms. Greene shares her home with 3 cats and 3 dogs. When her writing and pets allow it, she enjoys gardening, music, and doing volunteer work at her church.